Teens Speak
on Family Matters

Teens Speak
on Family Matters

Truth, Tension, Trials, and Triumphs

Edited by Laurie Delgatto

Saint Mary's Press®

 Genuine recycled paper with 10% post-consumer waste. 5102500

The publishing team included Laurie Delgatto, development editor; Jayne Zellers, editorial intern; Lorraine Kilmartin, reviewer; Mary Koehler, permissions editor; prepress and manufacturing coordinated by the prepublication and production services departments of Saint Mary's Press.

Printed in the United States of America

Printing: 9 8 7 6 5 4 3 2 1

Year: 2014 13 12 11 10 09 08 07 06

ISBN-13: 978-0-88489-875-7
ISBN-10: 0-88489-875-X

Library of Congress Cataloging-in-Publication Data

Teens speak on family matters : truth, tension, trials, and triumphs / edited by Laurie Delgatto.
     p. cm.
ISBN 0-88489-875-X (pbk.)
     1. Catholic teenagers—Religious life.
2. Catholic teenagers—Family relationships.
3. Family—Religious aspects—Catholic Church.
I. Delgatto, Laurie.
BX2355.T44 2006
248.8'3—dc22
                    2006009615

Dedication

For Brooke, Alyssa, and Erin. And for
Brigette, the heart of their family.

Acknowledgments

With a book like this one, we are limited to a certain number of
pages. All the writings we received are worthy of publication
because they speak of the wisdom that young people have to
offer one another and the world at large. We express gratitude
to all the young people who took the time to write and share
their thoughts.

So many youth ministers, religious educators, teachers, and
parents continually support our efforts to make the voices of
young people heard and known through books such as this
one. We extend our deepest thanks to those who encouraged
so many young people to put their words into writing and then
sent them on to us.

And finally, I wish to thank Mary Koehler and Jayne Zellers
for their assistance with this project.

—Laurie Delgatto

Foreword

There are many "hot button" words in our culture today and among them, I believe, is the word *family.* For some, the word brings fond experiences, memories, and feelings of joy-filled grace. For others, the mere mention of the word *family* brings pain, sorrow, bitterness, and deep-seated, everlasting scars.

These days family-life experts share their research, wisdom, and expertise—and for many, their latest book as well—on television, radio, Internet sites, and in our newspapers. They also are guest speakers at our churches and schools. So one might ask, Of what value is reading another book on family life?

Sometimes I think we all just need some honest, frank, and spiritual inspiration that can come from sources that vary greatly from our research-and-statistic-loving society. Sometimes I believe people of all ages and generations have a deep desire for someone to just give it to them straight, to share messages in ways that teach, inspire, challenge, and truly affect mind, soul, and body.

This book definitely gives us straight talk from young people in the form of thought-filled, honest, and insightful stories, poems, and reflections. God's grace pours through each story and poem. There is nothing like sharing "truth" about family life.

May your reading of the truths of the varied families mentioned in this book cause you to ponder, reflect, and come to peace with your own family. May God's healing grace transcend the pages of this book and leap into your soul, transforming you with increased courage as you continue to build your own family life—today, tomorrow, and for generations to come.

May the Lord bless all those who have shared their time and talents in writing this book, and for all those at Saint Mary's Press who had the insight to undertake such a vital piece of literature for all generations to read and take into their hearts.

—Doug Brummel

Introduction

Teens care deeply about family. This observation shouldn't surprise us. After all, what is more central, more important, and at times more painful than our family experiences? Who hasn't felt the sting of a parent's anger, the exhilaration of a fun adventure with a sibling, or the pain of losing a grandparent? Teens feel deeply, passionately, and honestly about all these relationships, often speaking in a louder voice and with more candor than do most adults.

Written by high-school-age teens, *Teens Speak on Family Matters: Truth, Tension, Trials, and Triumphs* offers a glimpse into the emotional peaks and valleys of teenagers' relationships with their families. Teens write with honesty, insight, and creativity as they share their firsthand realities of life within a family. The joys, challenges, highlights, and sorrows of family life as seen through the eyes of teen writers are included in this diverse collection of writings.

Each entry is as unique as the writer, and yet all these writings share a common thread: family matters!

All of us know that at times, family life can feel like a ride on a roller coaster, which climbs up and up and up the track and then plummets suddenly to the bottom. Difficult experiences such as divorce or a death in the family can make us feel as though we just left our stomach at the top of the roller coaster and our mind got lost somewhere around that last sudden and unexpected turn. Family life also has moments of sheer pleasure and exhilaration, such as celebrations and holidays, and we want to partake in those again and again. In equal measure are those moments when our families carry on at a slow and steady pace, moments when we can take a deep breath and know that "all is well," despite the highs and the lows.

The writings in this collection appear in random order to remind the reader that family life is filled with many twists and turns, tensions, trials, and triumphs.

The reflections you find in the remaining pages hold great truth. Savor the honesty, the poignancy, and the depth with which they are being shared.

Whether you laugh, cry, smile, or sigh as you read these pages, you are sure to appreciate the essential and timeless truth that family does, in fact, matter!

—Laurie Delgatto, Editor

All About Family

Family

In Young People's Words

Family consisting of friends
Family consisting of relatives
Filled sometimes with love
Filled sometimes with hate
The giving of care, the giving of compassion
Made up of mind, made up of body
Made up of blood, made up of spirit
Being born into one, being married into one
Being joined with one
Of getting together
Of special occasions
Of Christmas, of Thanksgiving, of Easter
Of weddings, of birthdays, of funerals
Fighting with each other
Only to be reconciled
Relaxing with each other
Of sitting, standing, talking
Activities with one another
Of playing, camping, cooking
Days filled with anxiety
Of trouble, of problems
Days filled with excitement
Of expectations, of changes
Sometimes being happy
Joy, love, laughter, smiles
Sometimes being sad
Woe, hate, tears, frowns
Of giving up selflessly—one's time, money, life
Of taking back selfishly—one's time, money, life
Of living as a family
Every day of your life

—Kimberly Adkins

Many people have different definitions of families. Family is a wonderful thing that you will always have. Family is composed of parents, brothers and sisters, aunts and uncles, grandparents, cousins, and friends. These are people you look up to for guidance. They are always there when you need someone to talk to—whether it is about serious stuff or just random funny stuff. Many holidays you spend with them. These will be great memories that you will have about your family. During these holidays, you will share many interesting conversations with them. These are long-lasting friendships you will gain. You will have your family around, and they are just like your friends and will always be there. You can share your deep, dark secrets with them, and they won't repeat them. They are definitely people you can trust with anything.

—Brittany Radden

What is family? Family is a group of people tied together with a strand of love. In all, family are those who love one another, no matter how hard it may be to do. We all have our battles, some over doing better in school, some over being grounded. Family is our peers—like me—who give one another advice to overcome the common battles. My advice consists of the topics of good things about being a family, death, and lessons taught to me by my parents.

There are many good things about being in a family. Family experiences are all different in many ways. Some families are small, some are big. Some have two parents, some have one, and in others, parents may not live with them. As families, we have traditions and celebrations of many different sorts. The unique qualities and even quirks make being a family easier and more fun.

Of course, we do not live forever on earth. Death occurs every minute of the day. Unfortunately, for every person who dies, there are family and friends who mourn. But there is a bright side. There is another precious gift that comes from death. That is life. With death, there will be babies born into your family. It is essential to know that the death of family members only means that they are physically gone. They are, however, forever in your mind and heart guiding you through life's numerous hurdles.

Lessons from those who love you are so important. My mother has always said you should never judge those you do not know. This means that others also have problems in life and that you should be respectful of them because you truly don't know their lives. This will always be close to my heart.

Families are all different, with no two the same. We all encounter tragedies and battles, but we must remember that the help of God and one another is as close as it could ever be. Just follow your heart and family's advice and you will enjoy family life.

—Thomas Buneo

Families come from many different religious backgrounds, from being a Buddhist to being a Christian. Many families spend time praying, even when eating a snack at the table or when having a Christmas feast. There is a famous quote that is true for all families; it is "A family that prays together stays together." I think that is true because you can become closer when you pray. If you pray together, you can get a better knowledge and understanding of one another. You will be able to help one another with their problems and rejoice with them in their happiness. My family always does intentions before a meal, so we know that someone's praying to God for help on a test, or if someone is just feeling down and needs some love. Our family becomes closer to one another when we pray. Should yours?

—Alicia Trautman

My family is proudly German. They eat hamburgers, bratwurst, and other various sausages and fillets typical of our German heritage. Well, typical of everyone except me. I am the first and only person in my family who is a vegetarian. That's right, a vegetarian in a burger-loving, bratwurst-devouring family.

I only became a vegetarian a week ago. I am a big advocate of animals, and I felt it was time to take my support a step further. I have tried being a vegetarian before and lasted only a week. The jokes about how long I'll last this time are not in short supply, and neither is the lack of support my family seems to express.

For example, during our typical Sunday grocery shopping, my mom and I perused the store together. She seemed unaware of my unease as she dawdled in the meat aisle and continued to suggest lunch foods with meat in them for me. She said she understood me when I tried to point out my discomfort. But I wanted to scream that if she *really* understood, she sure didn't show it.

With all these signs of little support, I wondered if my family cared about what I cared about. But then I realized that wasn't as important as the fact that they care about me. Even if it isn't so clear all the time, I know they support me.

They understand that I am growing up and figuring out who I want to be, and they *care*. That's what's important, not what's on their dinner plates.

—Malinda Frevert

Family Table

The great thing about family life is the sharing and caring it produces. Because I come from an Italian background, the values of family and togetherness play a huge role in my life. Perhaps the best example of our togetherness and sharing is that every Sunday my family sits for an early supper. Along with the potatoes and pasta, we pass around thoughts and share ideas on the weeks that have come and the weeks that have yet to come. "How was your day?" "How is the dinner?" are spoken at our family table. These questions are not asked through sheer curiosity. Rather, they are asked through compassion and the hope for goodness each family member displays.

Among the talk about what a particular supermarket has on sale this week and how the baby slept last night, there's a sense of love that circulates around the room with each spoken word. You certainly do not have to be Italian, or a part of my family, to recognize this overwhelming sense of love. I'm sure that every family has a certain sense of caring during family time after reflecting upon it and understanding its true value.

—Joseph Randazzo

During the Holidays

I live with my mom and my dad. My two older sisters have grown up and moved out. I am sixteen years old. I have a job and I go to school; I barely see my family anymore. I cherish any time that I have with my family. I love to see my family because it is such a rare occasion to see my whole family at the same time. I love holidays because that is the time all of us request off, and we all eat together. We just hang out and talk about what's happening to us and what's going on in our lives. During the holidays we sit around, watch movies, dance, or do something too sentimental for public view—like cry. My favorite time of the year is the holidays. It's not because of the presents or the food. It used to be, but now it's all about the people.

—Catherine Kirby

My Extended Family

Family is very important to me and my parents. I am very close with many of my extended family members. My mom's side of my family almost all live in or around Sioux Falls, South Dakota. My dad, mom, and I usually visit them about once every one to two months.

My extended family is very important to me because I am an only child. My cousins have become almost like siblings to me because we are so close and I do not have siblings. I look up to all my cousins who are older than me. I also try to be a good example for all of my younger cousins.

One of my cousins, Katie, is a year older than I am. She is one of my best friends, and I can talk to her about anything. I love how we are so close, because many of my friends barely know any of their cousins. I cannot imagine holidays and other celebrations without my extended family. They make those days fun for me.

I am also really close with my dad's side of the family, even though we do not see each other as much. They live all over the United States. We try to have a family reunion once every two years. I see my grandpa about three or four times a year. I also talk on the phone with my aunts and uncles a lot. I like being able to talk to them because I can ask them for advice and get a point of view on a subject that is different from the one my parents have.

Being close to both sides of my extended family is very important to me because I am able to have other people be important in my life, and I am able to talk to them about problems in my life. I value all of my extended family's advice and friendship.

—Cassie Dorland

You Don't Know

You don't know,
You don't know, but
You are my silent strength; I lean on you, oblivious to all.
You don't know, but
I think about you constantly. "What do you think about me?"
    "How will this affect you?" or
"Am I showing that I am proud of myself so you are proud of
    yourself?"
You don't know, but
I need you more than you need me; every question you ask,
    every piece of advice you need, you come to me.
I live for those sacred moments when you think you need me—
    you really don't need me—you know the answer, the right
    way; I just help you find it.
You are not as dependent as you think, give yourself more
    credit, you are worth it.
You two shape me, what I want to aspire to, and how I want
    others to see me, how I see me. I am who I am because of
    you.
You don't know, but
You two are my idols.
You are my brother and sister,
Different parents but the same environment.
I lean on you more than you know.
I love you, and you will be with me as far away as I travel; you
    will be there.
Thank you, I love you.

—Cheyanne Halverson

Game Over?

The stale scent of teenage boy assaults my nose, as my little sister and I step into our brother's room. I take note that although Teige had been gone for some time now, I could still smell his dirty clothes. As disgusting as it sounds, I feel rather comforted knowing that his presence still echoes throughout our home.

I click on the fuzzy TV screen and flip on the "ghetto" Nintendo. The familiar sound of the Mario theme song fills the room as Michelle and I giggle over our mistakes and follies in our feeble attempt to beat the game.

For a short period, time is suspended, and it seems that Teige is again with us. I can almost feel his weight make the mattress pull downward and hear his robust laughter mingling with ours.

For about the millionth time, I get a "Game Over." Reality hits with a sudden jolt as Michelle starts to freak over the lost time. "I have to go to dance in 10 minutes; I'll never get ready in time!" she practically shrieks as she hops from the overly high bed, running pell-mell out of the room. I take my time slipping from my seat. Turning off the game, I stare around the room. The bed is stripped bare, appearing like a maple tree in the heart of winter, cold and lonely. Once again, I think of my second-eldest brother. A wave of melancholy washes over my heart, and a film of tears fills my eyes. Then I remember that he will not be gone forever.

If he didn't make it back for Thanksgiving for sure, he would definitely be back for Christmas. College couldn't keep him forever, could it? It doesn't even have the "ghetto" Nintendo game that Michelle and I were having so much fun playing. Maybe when he comes back, we could all beat the game together? Maybe we will even let our eldest brother take a try when he comes home from college, too. Maybe.

—Christina Weidner

More Than Just Cousins

As a child I didn't get to see them that often because they constantly moved. I got so excited when they came to town. They always spent time with me and never let me feel left out. Now that I'm older, I realize they've taught me so many lessons that I'll carry with me throughout my life. My older cousins—Jennifer, Katie, Alex, and Mary—have significantly influenced my life.

I have a huge family and lots of cousins, but these four cousins have taught me the most. Each one has shown me how to live my life, though not always directly. Their actions alone taught me how to appreciate the blessings I have. I look up to them and want to live my life like they live theirs.

I look to Jen and Katie as the older sisters I never had. They took me to movies, the mall, and they always let me come to their homes. As a member of both of their weddings, I felt honored to have had that privilege. They taught me how to be a role model for the younger cousins that I have. Both have college degrees—Jennifer even completed law school—and they have managed to have families of their own. I hope to receive an excellent education and then have a wonderful family someday.

Alex, though I'm sure he doesn't realize it, has taught me to take life seriously. During his first year of college, he partied too much and flunked out of his school. I now know to take advantage of the wonderful educational opportunities I have. I need to keep my goals as the highest priority in life and not let temptations get in my way.

I chose Mary as my Confirmation sponsor because I spiritually look up to her. Mary's faith has influenced the person she has become; I need to always remember to put God first in my life. Mary reminds me that God will guide me on my life path.

My cousins have always supported me. They go above and beyond that of just cousins. Each has taught me different lessons in life. I keep their advice very close to my heart. They have helped shape the person I've become.

—Jessica Rose Garbe

Do Good

My grandma is my hero. I have several fond memories of her, and she has helped me become the person I am today. However, she was diagnosed with cancer seventeen months ago and my life was changed forever. After a courageous battle, she went to be with the Lord on May 14, 2004.

In the summer before my sophomore year, my family and I received the news that she had a rare form of cancer. In the following months, she survived two surgeries and chemotherapy, and my family and I were hoping for the best. Right before this past Christmas, however, the doctors told us her cancer counts were up.

Christmas was different that year. Instead of dwelling on the fact that we might never celebrate another Christmas with her in person, we didn't take the time we had for granted. We said an extra prayer at dinner for her health, took our time enjoying the food she had prepared, said an extra thank you after all the gifts had been opened, and exchanged a few additional "I love yous" as we departed for home.

On April 7, she was admitted to the hospital for the final time. On Easter morning, the doctor told us she was not going to be able to live to the end of the year. Only a few days later, she was moved to a hospice facility, with about thirty days to live. It was there that she spent her last birthday, her last Mother's Day, and where many other memories were created that will last a lifetime.

She passed away on May 14, 2004, around 2:15 p.m. My mom likes to say my grandma no longer has cancer. When I told her good-bye for the last time, I was going to school the day she died. I whispered to her that I had to go to school. As I bent down to give her one last hug, she replied by saying, "Okay, honey. Do good. I love you." Those words will stick with me for the rest of my life.

—Sara Mason

The Meaning of Family

Your family is always there for you,
They are the ones whose love is true.
Your family supports you no matter what you do.
They love you, care for you, and treasure you.
Family is there through thick and thin,
It does not matter to them if you lose or win.
They are there for you when you are ready to leave the nest.
Having your family near is always the best.
You can come home to them when you are feeling homesick.
Family is always the number-one pick.
Family is there to help in showing you the way,
They will never lead you astray.
Having a family is God's greatest gift.
They will always give your spirit a lift.
Your family always knows how to make you smile,
They will go that extra mile.
So, always thank God for your family
Because they are always there for you and me.

—Julie Yost

Verses of Youth

Going up the steel elevator,
Listening to soft music play.
I'm really bored and curious how
This is supposed to be a happy day?

Our little posse exits onto floor five,
Our shoes squeaking on the newly waxed floor.
We walk down the hallway
And proceed through a door.

My mom is in her bed,
And smiles as we come in.
She starts to talk to us,
Asking how we've been.

After some time, she pops the question:
Would we like to hold her?
But she looks at me, not Sarah,
Because, of course, I'm older.

I sit in a plastic chair, prepared
To hold the brand new baby.
Then I start to think with horror
That I might drop her (maybe).

Now I'm feeling scared
As they hand her to me.
"Katie," they say, smiling,
"This is your new sister, Becky."

Becky opens her eyes and looks up at me,
She is so pink and small.
Then the special moment is gone,
And the baby starts to bawl.

I start to panic,
And when my dad comes near,
I thrust her into his arms
As he comforts us both, saying, "It's okay, dear."

After she settles down,
And becomes mute once more,
We say good-bye to mom,
And exit, leaving the fifth floor.

Downstairs, outside,
And back into the Saab.
Traveling down the street, I think,
"I have a brand new job."

She is my new sister, Becky,
A second sibling for me.
And although I give a conflicting impression,
To be her big sister, I am quite happy.

—Katie White

Does He Remember?

Does he remember my first soccer game?
Does he remember my gymnastics class?
What about the time I ran away?
Or the time he broke that glass?
Does he remember Tanya?
We used to play all the time.
What about Seth or Katie?
They were good friends of mine.
Does he remember that night they took me?
When our family took me away from him?
They put all my things in bags and that's when he knew.
That was the night his world would go dim.
Does he remember how I cried?
And yelled at them to leave me alone?
They told me dad needed help,
And after he got it, he would come home.
Does he remember any of this?
I'm not really sure, but I do.

These things run through my memory,
And I can only wonder if they run through his, too.
Even though these past thoughts I will remember,
He will always be my hero.
The way he's turned around,
He makes the other dads look like a zero.
Will he remember the things that happen now?
One would only think
Because now he has learned,
His problems cannot be solved with a drink.

—Megan Morrison

What is the best thing about being part of a family? Is it getting all the presents at Christmas and other special occasions? No, it is not. The best thing about being part of a family is knowing that you will always be loved. Your race, your size, or your age don't matter. Someone will always be there to tell you they love you. Someone will always be there to lend a shoulder for you to cry on. Someone will always be there to comfort you when you are down. When you feel like you are alone in this world and that no one understands you, someone will be there telling you that you are not alone and that they do understand you. It could be your mom, your dad, your grandparents, or one of your siblings, but no matter what, someone will always be there.

—Sabrina Anania

Living in 2004, I've grown into a strong girl with many morals. But my parents don't see that! I'm from the Middle East and born in the United States; I've learned that life is different in both parts of the world. Because I'm a Jordanian living here, my parents treat me differently, keeping a closer eye on me. They have no faith in me because of the peer pressure that's always there. My parents don't think I know what to do in bad situations, so they keep me from experiencing the normal things teenagers go through. Born in the 1960s, my parents don't understand the way of life as the years have gone by. They think that many bad things can come out of the United States.

My parents also don't realize that some situations are difficult to avoid. Yes, there are drugs and, yes, there are people who drink and smoke, but that doesn't mean that I follow in their footsteps. I've learned responsibility from the two people that don't know that I take them into consideration. I'm responsible and have always given full attention to the phrase "Drinking, drugs, and smoking is bad for you." I will never do any of the sorts, just because I know it's not healthy for my body and for the people who love me. It's reassuring to know that people, like me, out there still have respect for themselves to not hurt their bodies.

Since my parents are strict, my limitations on what I can do with friends have increased. They don't allow me to wear clothing like others do, and I don't have normal curfews or punishments. I can't talk to boys on the phone or talk to them on the weekends; they aren't allowed to come into my house and vice versa. My parents judge my friends as they walk into my house, so I've given up on letting them meet my parents. Mom tells me that I can't go out with people she doesn't know. Well, if she judges my friends, how is she supposed to know who they are?

—Lisa Ghazi Sawaged

Love and Hate

I grew up in a small town in Iowa. I had a mother, a father, and a little sister. I thought my family was like everyone else's, and it was—on the outside. Yet on the inside, away from the eyes of others, it was another story. You see my parents didn't get along. Many of my childhood memories are of one fight or another. They did try, though. They went to marriage counseling and worked out a few of their problems. Then things were as they should be for a while, but a few days later, the fighting returned. Now, this routine continued until I was about eight. When on a beautiful summer evening, I heard the word *divorce* for the first time. At the age of eight, I didn't know what that word meant, but I did know what the words "Daddy is moving out and won't be living with us anymore" meant.

At the sound of those words, my whole world fell apart. My parents were splitting up, my life was changing before my eyes, and I couldn't do anything about it. All I could do, though, was stare at what was happening as though I were a bystander instead of a main character.

For a time, things were miserable. I missed my dad, my mom always worked, and I kept blaming myself. Those around me said that it wasn't my fault, but it didn't help. I was sure that if I had been a better daughter, they would have stayed together.

Now, as I look back, I realize that part of my life was a time of learning and emotional growth. Thinking about the fighting doesn't hurt as bad because I now know that had my parents stayed together, I probably wouldn't be who I am today. Because even though my parents never physically hurt me, emotionally—because of the fighting and hatred—I was bruised and bloody. Had they stayed together that hatred would have seeped into my being and become a permanent part of me.

—Sarah A. Marsh

Loving God,

You sent your saints and other holy people to be living examples for me. Help me recognize the importance of these men and women and the many lessons I can learn from them. Let these models of faith teach me how to act, especially when it comes to matters of my family.

Although it is often difficult to do so, help me recognize the many talents of my brothers and sisters. Rather than be critical, allow me to offer guidance, support, and recognition for their wonderful gifts.

Thomas More understood the many sacrifices that a parent must make for his children. He always put his children before himself and would sacrifice anything for their sake. Help me recognize the countless sacrifices my parents make for me. Also, although we may have varying opinions, help me understand that whatever my parents do, they are doing it to help me become a better person of faith.

Abraham was ready and willing to sacrifice his own son to please you. Please let me be willing to do the same for my family. Although I may be ridiculed and criticized, allow me to be willing to do anything for my family, at any given time. Your son, Jesus Christ, died for me. Likewise, allow me to be willing to do the same for my family.

Lord, help me make my family the most important part of my life.

Amen.

—John Thomas Kyler

Headlights in the Rearview Mirror

Turning sixteen is a milestone for most teenage girls. It signifies freedom and independence. I know I felt that way the first few months of turning sixteen. Having a car and driving myself to places felt so liberating. My parents' concern for my safety grew a lot those first few months. They were leery about letting me drive myself to school.

I remember when my older brother turned sixteen and was able to drive from place to place. My mom and I wouldn't leave the house until we saw my brother awake and walking down the stairs ready to leave. My parents had a strong feeling that if he were left at home to get ready for school by himself, he'd have a horrible attendance record at school.

When the time came for me to want to drive, my parents thought it would still be wise for me to leave at the same time as my mom. I thought nothing of it. For the past three months, it has been the same routine. I am the first to pull out of the driveway, and my mom follows behind me. She stays behind me while on the interstate, until the time comes when I exit onto Forty-second Street, and she continues straight toward downtown. But some mornings, I lose her headlights in my rearview mirror. I get anxious and wonder if she's caught in traffic while I squeeze through. But those Jeep headlights always reassure me. I may lose them for a moment, but they always reappear. Every time I look in my mirror, I see her there and sometimes feel comforted by those headlights. Those headlights remind me of how much my parents have always been behind me. Riding a bicycle for the first time, I knew that their hands were on my seat, making sure I didn't waver. I can always look behind me and see them there. I may think that I've lost them, but it takes just one look to prove myself wrong.

—Katie Cook

Dear Diary,

Now that I finally feel that my life is moving at a pace that I can once again handle, I have decided to sit down and reflect on this whole incident. The past few weeks, months, years have been ones I will never forget. They are full of many memories, some of which are good, but unfortunately, also many I would like to forget. But I know they are memories I will never be able to forget—and also ones I should not forget.

To me, in July of 1999 when he came from Seattle to live with us and start a life here in Colorado, my Uncle Mike was everything. He was my dad's brother and the uncle I never really knew I had, the big brother I always wanted, and the dad that my dad couldn't always be. He loved cooking and created awesome dishes for dinner; he took my sisters and me out to the movies, and no matter what, he always kidded around with me. For those six months that my Uncle Mike lived in our basement, I was one of the happiest kids around. Whenever Mike went out, I went with him if I could. Whenever we all went camping, instead of driving with my own family, I drove with Mike. Whenever I was home and had nothing to do, I hung out with Mike. We laughed for hours until our bellies hurt and we were rolling on the ground crying. I grew to be closer to Mike in that short time period than to any other family member I had. I wasn't sure why, but for some reason, Mike was sort of a hero to me, and I was proud to call him my uncle.

But are things ever as great as they seem? Many heroes have their weak points and Mike was not perfect either. In January of 2000 he moved into his own apartment, and soon another side of Mike that had been hidden from me began to show. As lies unfolded and the truth about suspicious matters began to show, I slowly began to understand why Mike had come to Colorado to "start a new life." My Uncle Mike was an alcoholic. But as the saying goes, "Once an alcoholic always an alcoholic." My family discovered that even before he began living with us, Mike had started drinking again. As tales of drunken nights, SWAT teams, and jail time were unveiled, I began to see my hero crumble before me. Time passed and suddenly Mike was adding new chapters to his life story. He spent countless nights drunk at home, frequently in hospital beds, and even in jail.

By April of 2002, my once rock-hard superman had deteriorated into a pile of dust. I no longer trusted him, respected him, or even liked him. He had lied to my family, put us all through unneeded nights and days of worry, and missed my last two birthdays because he had been in the hospital or rehab. But most of all, he had trashed the relationship between him and me that I had treasured so dearly. While the rest of my family and our friends continued trying to clean him up, I shunned him. He had critically hurt my family and my ability to trust people. I no longer answered the phone when he called or talked to him when he came over. I didn't want anything to do with him, and he knew it.

My Uncle Mike committed suicide on June 28, 2002. He did it when my parents and I were all out of town. My cousin received the call at our home while she was taking care of my sisters and immediately contacted my parents, bringing them home from their business meeting in New Orleans. I, however, was in Belize and had no idea what had happened.

I returned home on July 2, exhausted but running on adrenaline from the excitement of having just experienced the trip of a lifetime. But my giddy emotions were soon shattered and replaced with tears of sorrow as my parents told me the news. As the next few days passed, I experienced feelings of mourning, relief, and regret. I had lost my uncle, but for the first time in a while, he was finally at peace. The hardest thing for me to cope with was the fact that I had never gotten to forgive him for what he had done or to tell him once more that I did truly love him.

I have learned more life lessons from Mike then any other person, and he didn't even know he was teaching me. But the two biggest lessons I have learned from Mike are obvious. I don't need someone to tell me not to do drugs or to drink just to be cool because I know that it can hurt not only me but also my family and friends. Alcohol is not worth the price you and your family pay just for a little "harmless fun." And he taught me that good people do bad things. My Uncle Mike didn't mean to hurt the people he loved the most, but his problems were too much for him to handle, and unfortunately those burdens weighed down his entire family. I think about Mike every day and ask God why it had to be my uncle's death that I learned from, but I also realize that some things are just meant to be. I cannot change the fact that Mike is dead, but I can use his story and learn from his mistakes.

It has now been two years since Mike died, and I can finally say that I am at peace with Mike. Instead of cursing at him for the pain he put me through, I now talk to him and thank him for the wonderful things he brought into my life. Mike made me a stronger and more mature person. I still talk to him and even laugh at him. I won't be able to bust a gut with him anymore, but I always know that he is there for me. He has become my guardian angel. And I can't think of any better angel to have than my Uncle Mike.

—Margaret Louise Munson

My idea of family is a large group of people who love one another. My family fits this description very well. My family often is like any other family. There are awesome times in my family when we get along great, but there are times when we fight horribly. This is what makes families so great. Family members are people you can always go to with your problems and trust them to be honest. This is what is awesome about families. You can always be yourself around them, and they accept you for who you are. Family are the people who know you best and love you despite all of your flaws. This is what I love most about my family.

My family is one of the most important things in my life and what keeps me going every day. Without my family I would be lost. My family is my anchor and my support. Because my family is so big, there is always someone to talk to or just hang out with. Family is so important to me because it is where you learn so much before you start school. Parents are your first teachers of religion. Your siblings are your first friends and the ones you are always closest to.

Something great about having a large family is that there are so many different qualities in my brothers and sisters. That means there is always someone to turn to if I need advice, if I need cheering up, or if I just want to have fun. All my siblings are so different and unique, but we all get along fairly well. My life would be so difficult without my family.

I cannot imagine life without my parents and siblings. Life would be so dull without them. Family is what forms you into who you are and what you will become. It is who you share everything with. You share clothes, rooms, secrets, and memories with your family. I would be nothing without my family and I am so grateful for them.

—Libby Slater

A Family Torn Apart by Death

When my grandpa died over a year ago, it was really hard on my dad and his three older brothers, along with his younger sister. He was about seventy-four when he was first put into a nursing home because he couldn't take care of himself without help. A month earlier my grandma fell off the roof of their house and seriously hurt herself and lost her speech and ability to walk. She stayed in the hospital for four months. That had really put stress on him.

Darwin was his name and Virginia was hers. She was seventy-three when she was in the hospital, and she was later released to where my grandpa was staying. They were happy that they were together in the same place; it isn't that big of a place. She died in December, a week before Christmas. We went through the whole deal of gathering all our relatives and planning for the funeral. It was a tearjerker. But it was nice that everyone got to see one another.

My grandpa, who was still living in the nursing home, died in March. He died the day before their anniversary, and my grandma died two days after his birthday. Everyone noticed that when we were making a card for people to let them know about my grandparents' childhoods.

Their will said that the family could split the money five ways among them all. They could decide what to do with all the other stuff from the house. They could choose what to do with the house. They decided to put the house up for rent along with all of the farmland. A lovely family is living there and doing all the farm work.

Since they died, we all have lost contact with the family, so I don't really know what all my cousins are doing. It's torn us apart to not know what everyone is doing. It would be nice to see them and how everyone has grown.

—Mallory DeLong

The best thing about being part of a family is that there will always be someone who loves me and someone I will always love. Just because some family members do not show that they love one another does not mean they do not love one another.

An example of this is when my siblings and I argue, which is constantly. Sometimes they argue with me for the better—to get me not to do something that could ruin my life—and I take that for granted sometimes and brush it off my shoulder. They are doing this because they love me and are watching out for me.

An example is my parents and I. When I make a bad decision, hang out with people who are not the best influences, or when I made a mistake in general, they let nature run its course to get me to learn from what I have done wrong. They do this because they love me and do not want me to make the same decision again.

My family has grown so much from loving one another and taking the advice we give to one another and learning from it. I think that if I were put with a different family, I would never be able to love them as much as I love the family I have. My mother and father taught my sisters, brother, and me how to love and to grow in love.

—Mary Elster

Memory

Memories are what link us to the past and give us hope for the future; however, if you do not have a functioning memory, then your life just turns into blurred recollections that do not always make sense. Both of my grandparents on my father's side of the family have lost their memories. They have Alzheimer's disease.

Their memories are lost, forgotten in sands of time.
They don't come back, no matter how far they reach into their
    mind.
The look on my daddy's face when one of them forgets his
    name
Has left me so sad, not in the least bit the same.
It's so difficult to cope with the pain I feel
When all seems so lost and not even real.
My grandpa has lost his ability to speak,
Making the situation even more bleak.
My grandma has just been put into a nursing room,
A room that, quite frankly, resembles a tomb.
I love my grandparents with all my heart and soul,
And they taught me something that has become an important
    goal:
A memory is not for certain; live your life so everything will
    stand out and will have to be remembered because it was
    so great.

—Laura Bruce

Grandparents

Respect your elders. This phrase may be one that is forgotten in our society, which shuns those who are "old and gray." We prefer to put them away, locked up in a nursing or retirement home so our fast-paced lives may continue. However, does not slow-and-steady win the race?

My grandparents are such a strong hold in my life that I disregard society, and I love keeping them in my thoughts, actions, and prayers. My grandparents have had such a large and positive impact on my life that I believe I would be a different woman than I am today if they were never in my life.

My grandma Jeanne Gonderinger lost her husband, my grandfather Norman Gonderinger, before I was born. The only picture in my mind of my Grandma Jeanne is a strong woman, with a strength and inner glow that radiates out to all those around her. Throughout her life she has been through so much and has ample amounts of wisdom to share. I question society by asking why one would ever want to shut out such knowledge.

My mother's parents, William and Marilyn Mattern, also have had a large impact on my life. Grandma Marilyn delivered eight children, and Grandpa Bill worked hard to send all eight of those children to a Catholic grade school and high school, as well as college. Together they have shown me that God will always find a way, and to never lose hope in any situation. Grandpa Bill also fought in World War II, and never in my life have I heard him mention any stories from his experiences there. However, this past summer my grandfather was sitting down, and he began to tell me a timeline of his war experience. To me this was like a child receiving a Christmas present, and yet all I was receiving was a story.

When we shut out our elders, especially those in our family, we lose important wisdom and stories that can be passed down through generations. So, the next time you are moving in our fast-paced society, remember: Respect your elders.

—Jesse Anne Gonderinger

A Miracle Family

The two miracles in my family are about my brother and me. God knew he could not give my mom two kids with problems, so he took one of the problems away, and that was mine. My fifteen-year-old brother was born with autism. He is my miracle.

This is his miracle story: As far back as I can remember, I have always said, "Charlie, don't touch that" or "Charlie, stay behind me." These sayings have become implanted into my head. Not being allowed to say "shhh" or touching his shirt is what I have grown up with. "What is wrong with your brother?" is a question I am always asked. When I was little and did not know what to reply, I always told people that he was special and needed extra attention. But that is just the thing: he *is* special. It took a lot of growing up to realize that. I could not ever imagine having a "normal" little brother. Being a big sister, I have become extremely overprotective of him.

This is my miracle story: I was born with cystic fibrosis, a fatal genetic disease in which mucus builds up in the lungs. The doctors said I was only supposed to live to see my teenage years. My mother attended Mass one night at Holy Ghost, and the sermon that night happened to be on healing. During the consecration, the priest stopped Mass and said, "Someone is praying for a healing right now."

During Communion, my brother, who was a baby at the time, was being loud and crying in the Communion line. After Mass, the priest approached my mom and asked her if she was the one with the fussy baby. He then told her that he heard a voice say, "That's the one, that's the family." My mom then had tests run on me; they came out negative, saying that I was cured. Nobody has ever been able to explain this story, except for my mom who has had a strong faith her whole life. God knew what he was doing.

—Mollie Wyskowski

Family, a word so small yet full of meaning.
A family instills values beginning at youth,
Starting as early as losing one's baby tooth,
Values that will guide one through the journey of life.
Supporting one through all the misfortunes and strife,
A family works together in order to achieve unity.
However, individuals may work hard to seek their own
    opportunities.
Family is the backbone of every neighborhood,
They show generosity, as everyone should.
They are the link to the past generations,
They help us remain without separation,
They pass down traditions,
And help us complete our lifelong missions.
Families share stories of wisdom, laughter, and adversity.
They give us culture and encourage the spread of diversity.
They give us strength during difficult times,
From scraping our knees to overcoming crimes.
Family gives us a foundation upon which we build our lives.
When God inspires us through our family, we may thrive.

—Julienne Vicens

Lord,

I know we are supposed to love those who love us.

I know we are supposed to respect those who have given
themselves to help us.

I know we are supposed to treat others as we would want them
to treat us.

You know we don't always do that.

You know we talk back, swear, and disrespect those we should
love.

You know we could do more for our parents.

Please help us be more loving, caring, and understanding.

Help us be more like Mary, who raised you and is the absolute
model of love and compassion.

Help those of us who struggle with family issues that destroy
this union of love and growth.

Help us took past the small conflicts and look at what our
parents have sacrificed for us.

Please help us be more like you and your mother.

Amen.

—Matthew Sauvage

Prayer for My Family—My Inspiration and My Love

Loving God,
You have given me a life of love that flows and never ends,
You have given me my family, a group of close and faithful
    friends.
You have given me my softhearted mother to watch my every
    stride,
You have given me my devoted father in whom I can confide.
You have given me my cheerful sisters who can always make
    me chuckle,
You have given me your enduring strength when I feel as
    though I will buckle.
You have given me a family on whom I can depend,
You have given me a family, which I will defend.
You have given me the remarkable people to complete my life,
You have given me the only ones who can carry off my strife.
Lord, I want to thank you for your generosity and never-ending
    charity,
You have sent me an irreplaceable family to give me a calming
    sense of clarity.

—Michele Formico

Your Thoughts
on Family

Use the questions, suggestions, and the space provided on the following pages to help you capture your own thoughts, ideas, and feelings about family life.

o   What is your definition of family?

_____

_____

_____

_____

_____

_____

_____

_____

_____

o   Share about something (a trait, a possession, words
     of wisdom) that has been passed down through the
     generations in your family.

_____

_____

_____

_____

_____

_____

_____

_____

_____

o   What is the best thing about being part of a family?

_____

_____

_____

_____

_____

_____

_____

_____

_____

o   What is the most difficult thing about being part of
     a family?

_____

_____

_____

_____

_____

_____

_____

_____

_____

o   What is your favorite family story or memory?

_____

_____

_____

_____

_____

_____

_____

_____

_____

o   Describe a difficult time for your family and how you
    (and your family) overcame it.

_____

_____

_____

_____

_____

_____

_____

_____

_____

_____

o   How has divorce or separation affected you and
your family?

_____

_____

_____

_____

_____

_____

_____

_____

_____

o   How has the death of a family member affected you
and your family?

_____

_____

_____

_____

_____

_____

_____

_____

_____

o What is one thing about parents that you wish you could understand better?

_____

_____

_____

_____

_____

_____

_____

_____

_____

o What is the greatest lesson your mother or your father (or both parents) has taught you?

_____

_____

_____

_____

_____

_____

_____

_____

_____

o   Discuss the kind of pressure you experience as the oldest (youngest, middle) child in your family.

_____

_____

_____

_____

_____

_____

_____

_____

o   How has faith and religion affected or shaped your family life?

_____

_____

_____

_____

_____

_____

_____

_____

_____

o   Why is it sometimes easier to talk openly with a
    friend than with a parent or other family member?

_____

_____

_____

_____

_____

_____

_____

_____

_____

o   How have your grandparents influenced you?

_____

_____

_____

_____

_____

_____

_____

_____

_____

_____

o   Why are extended families (and extended family members) important?

_____

_____

_____

_____

_____

_____

_____

_____

o   What values has your family modeled that you like to, or would like to, imitate in your own life?

_____

_____

_____

_____

_____

_____

_____

_____

o   How has illness or disability affected your family?

_____

_____

_____

_____

_____

_____

_____

_____

_____

o   What have you learned from a brother or a sister?

_____

_____

_____

_____

_____

_____

_____

_____

_____

_____

o   What is the best experience you have had in praying
together as a family?

_____

_____

_____

_____

_____

_____

_____

_____

o   What struggles do you have over religious beliefs or
practices?

_____

_____

_____

_____

_____

_____

_____

_____

_____

o   What are the things you argue about with your parents? Why do you think these things are the source of conflict?

_____

_____

_____

_____

_____

_____

_____

_____

_____

_____

_____

_____

_____

_____

_____

_____

_____

_____

_____

_____

_____

_____

Use the space on the following pages to create your own writings or poems on your feelings about family and family life.